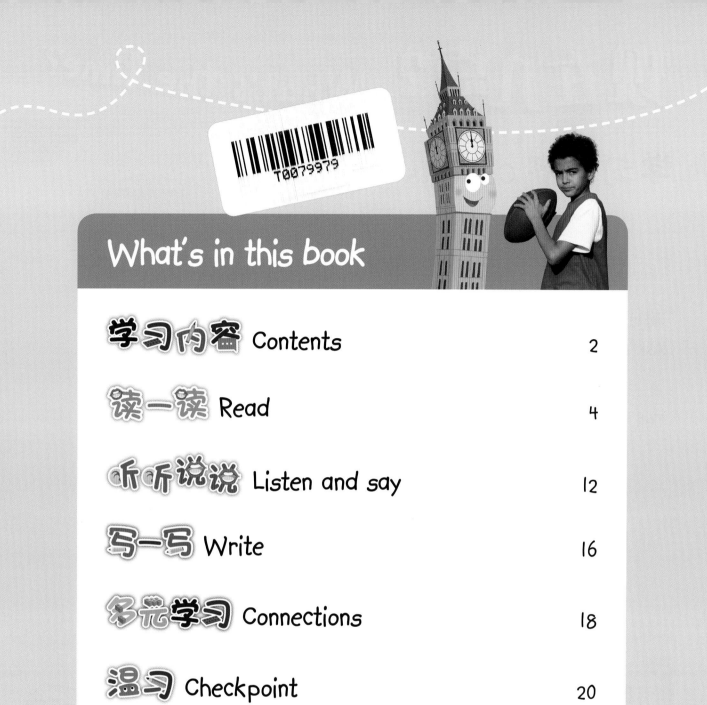

What's in this book

This book belongs to

_____

现在几点? What's the time?

学习内容 Contents

沟通 Communication

询问时间
Ask about the time

表示时间
Tell the time

生词 New words

⭐	早上	early morning
⭐	上午	morning
⭐	下午	afternoon
⭐	晚上	evening, night
⭐	现在	now
⭐	两	two
⭐	点	o'clock
⭐	半	half
⭐	分	minute
	中午	noon
	号	date

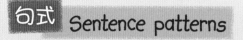 **Sentence patterns**

现在几点？
What's the time?

现在早上八点半。
It is 8:30 in the morning.

 **Project**

了解时区的概念，计算时差
Learn about time zones and calculate time differences

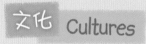 **Cultures**

古代中国时辰
The hours in ancient China.

Get ready

1 What time does your school start?

2 How often do you check the time in a day?

3 Do you know what 'time zone' means?

xiàn zài jǐ diǎn
现在几点？

上午十点半。

zǎo shang bàn
早上八点半。

现在几点？

xià wǔ
下午四点半。

wǎn shang
晚上九点半。

6

早上六点十五分。
fēn

上午九点十五分。

晚上七点四十五分。

晚上十点十五分。

下午两点十五分。
liǎng

一天有二十四小时。
一小时有六十分钟。

现在几点？你在哪里？
你在做什么？

Let's think

1 Look at the time and match the clocks.

2 Tell your friend which type of clock you like and why.
Design your clock on the right.

Analogue clock

Digital clock

New words

🎧 02 **1** Learn the new words.

中午   十 五 一 月   号

早上   点

上午   半

下午   分   两

晚上   现在

2 Look at the time and write the letters. You may use the letters more than once.

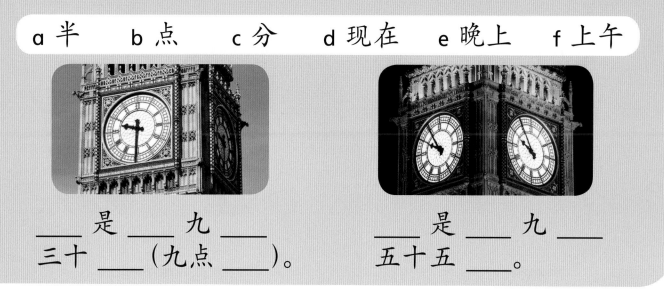

a 半   b 点   c 分   d 现在   e 晚上   f 上午

____ 是 ____ 九 ____ 三十 ____（九点 ____）。

____ 是 ____ 九 ____ 五十五 ____。

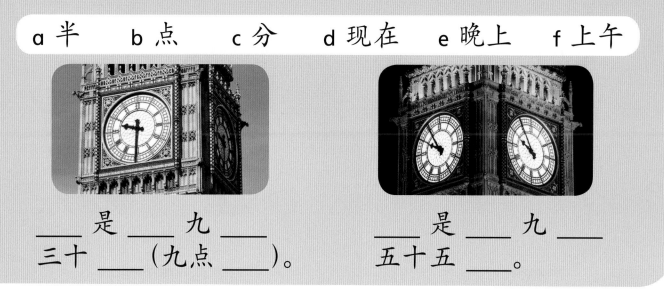

🎧 03 **1** Listen and mark the time on the clocks.

🎧 04 **2** Look at the pictures. Listen to the sto

1

2

3

4

nd say.

3 Match the sentences to the pictures. Say to your friend.

a　他们下午四点半看书。
b　她们上午十一点画画。
c　他们下午三点十五分踢足球。

Task

Talk about your daily routines and activities with your friend. Complete the table.

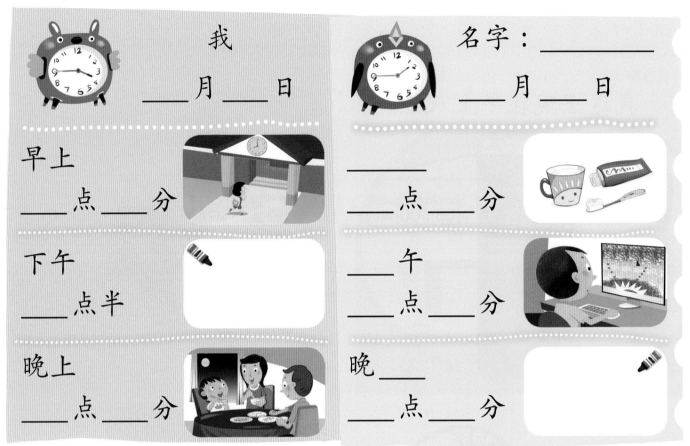

Game

Listen to your friend and act out the time.

9:30

12:00

2:15

2:00

7:45

3:30

8:15

10:45

Song

Listen and sing.

现在几点？

现在一点、两点、三点、四点。

现在几点？

现在五点半、六点半、七点半、八点半。

现在几点？

现在九点、十点、十一点、十二点。

课堂用语 Classroom language

两人一组。
Two people form a group.

四人一组。
Four people form a group.

1 Review and trace the strokes.

`	刁	ㄥ	く	し

2 Learn the component. Trace ⺌ to complete the characters.

⺌　点　燕　能　糕

3 Write the time in Chinese and the missing dots. How many dots are missing?

_____ 点

_____ 点

两点

五点

_____ 占

_____ 点

4 Trace and write the character.

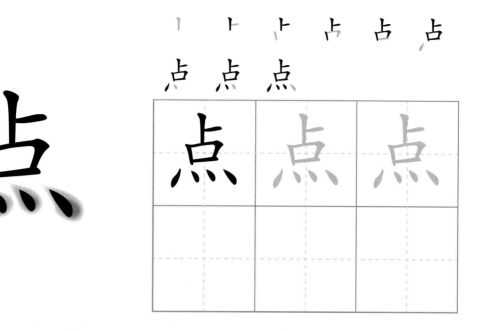

丶 卜 上 占 占

点 点 点

The same character can have more than one meaning.

Discuss the meanings of the characters in red with your friend.

你在哪里？
Indicate location.

三点

十分

你在做什么？
Indicate an activity/
action you are doing

三点

十分

Cultures

1 Learn about the hours in ancient China. Colour the first two-hour period red and the last one blue.

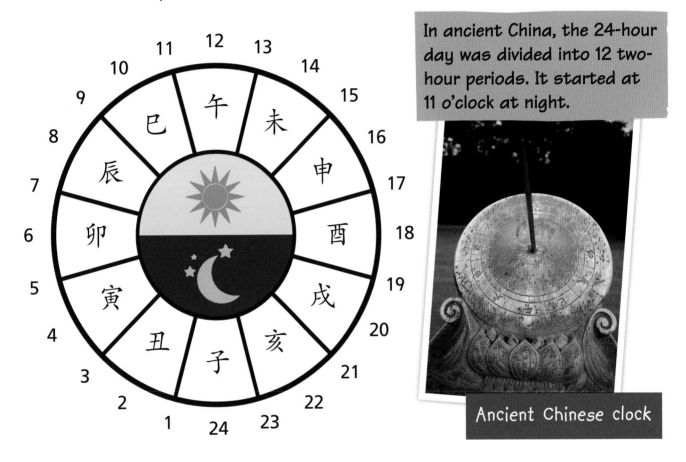

In ancient China, the 24-hour day was divided into 12 two-hour periods. It started at 11 o'clock at night.

Ancient Chinese clock

2 How many of your classmates were born at each of the two-hour period? Write the numbers in Chinese.

23-1	1-3	3-5	5-7	7-9	9-11	11-13	13-15	15-17	17-19	19-21	21-23
子	丑	寅	卯	辰	巳	午	未	申	酉	戌	亥

What's the time? Write below and report.

The Earth is divided into 24 time zones starting from the prime meridian.

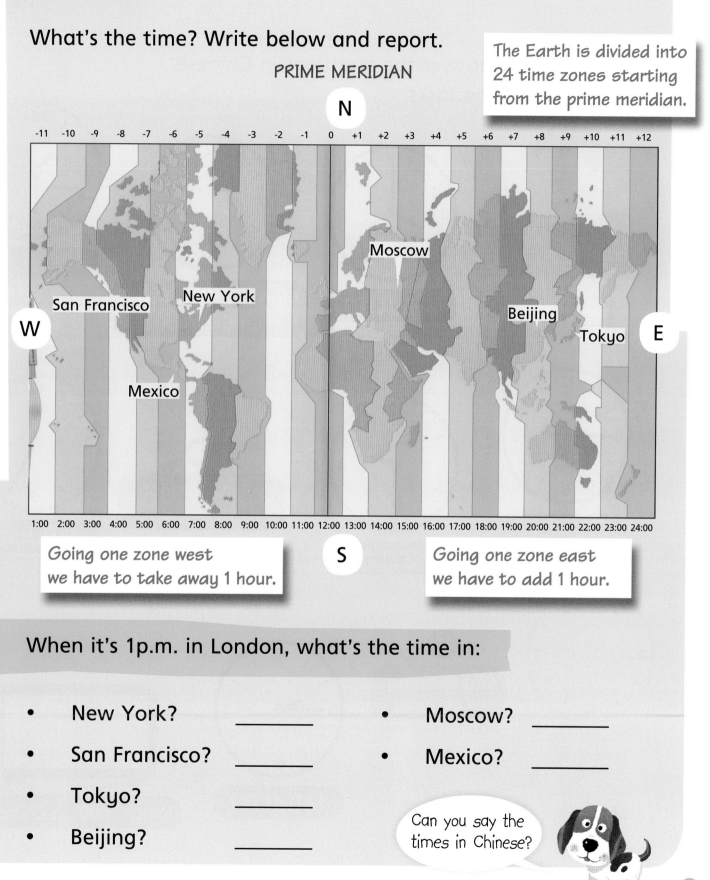

PRIME MERIDIAN

Going one zone west we have to take away 1 hour.

Going one zone east we have to add 1 hour.

When it's 1p.m. in London, what's the time in:

- New York? _____
- Moscow? _____
- San Francisco? _____
- Mexico? _____
- Tokyo? _____
- Beijing? _____

Can you say the times in Chinese?

温习 Checkpoint

Help Hao Hao answer the questions in Chinese and complete the tasks.

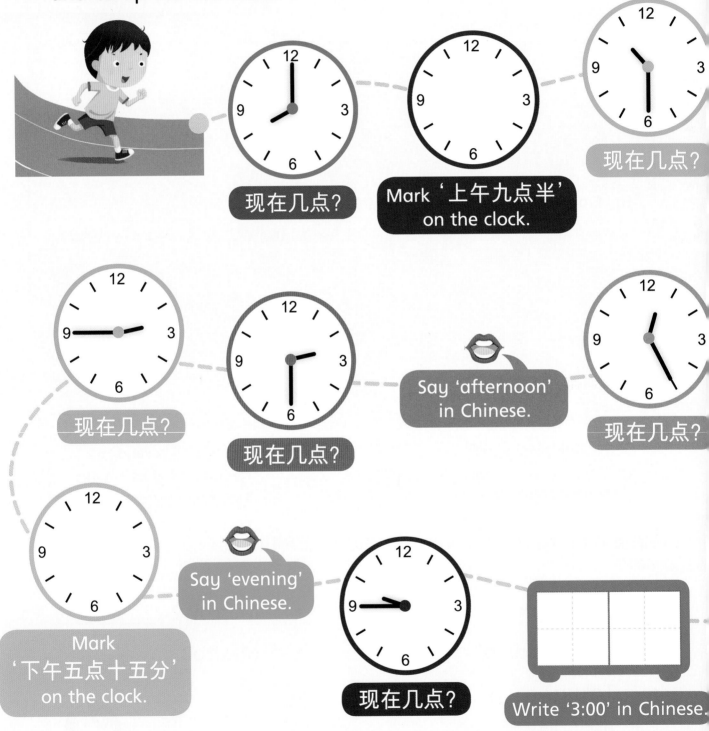

现在几点?

Mark '上午九点半' on the clock.

现在几点?

现在几点?

现在几点?

Say 'afternoon' in Chinese.

现在几点?

Mark '下午五点十五分' on the clock.

Say 'evening' in Chinese.

现在几点?

Write '3:00' in Chinese.

现在几点?

Mark '中午十二点' on the clock.

Write 'What's the time?' in Chinese.

2 Work with your friend. Colour the stars and the chilies.

Words and sentences	说	读	写
早上	☆	☆	☆
上午	☆	☆	🌶
下午	☆	☆	🌶
晚上	☆	☆	🌶
现在	☆	☆	🌶
两	☆	☆	🌶
点	☆	☆	☆
半	☆	☆	🌶
分	☆	☆	🌶
中午	☆	🌶	🌶
天	☆	☆	🌶
现在几点?	☆	☆	🌶
现在早上八点半。	☆	☆	🌶

Ask about the time	☆
Tell the time	☆

3 What does your teacher say?

分享 Sharing

Words I remember

早上	zǎo shang	early morning
上午	shàng wǔ	morning
下午	xià wǔ	afternoon
晚上	wǎn shang	evening, night
现在	xiàn zài	now
两	liǎng	two
点	diǎn	o'clock
半	bàn	half
分	fēn	minute
中午	zhōng wǔ	noon
号	hào	date

Other words

小时	xiǎo shí	hour
分钟	fēn zhōng	minute (as in duration)
在	zài	(to indicate an action in progress)
做	zuò	to do

OXFORD
UNIVERSITY PRESS

Oxford University Press is a department of the University of Oxford.
It furthers the University's objective of excellence in research, scholarship,
and education by publishing worldwide. Oxford is a registered trade mark of
Oxford University Press in the UK and in certain other countries

Published in Hong Kong by
Oxford University Press (China) Limited
39th Floor, One Kowloon, 1 Wang Yuen Street, Kowloon Bay,
Hong Kong

Illustrated by Anne Lee, Doris Lee, KK Ng, KY Chan and Wildman

Photographs for reproduction permitted by Dreamstime.com

China National Publications Import & Export (Group) Corporation is an authorized distributor of
Oxford Elementary Chinese.
Please contact content@cnpiec.com.cn or 86-10-65856782

ISBN: 978-0-19-942983-7

10 9 8 7 6 5 4 3 2